Claude the Tiger

A Division of The McGraw·Hill Companies

Columbus, Ohio

www.sra4kids.com

SRA/McGraw-Hill

A Division of The **McGraw·Hill** *Companies*

Send all inquiries to:
SRA/McGraw-Hill
8787 Orion Place
Columbus, OH 43240-4027

ISBN 0-07-569931-1
5 6 7 8 9 DBH 05

Maude has a pet tiger. Its name is Claude.
Claude's paws have sharp claws. But Maude is
glad she bought Claude.

"Claude is really tame," said Maude.
"I have taught him some tricks."

Paul watched Claude draw and tumble.
Claude caught every ball in a game of catch.
"Claude must be awfully smart.
What makes him smart, Maude?" asked Paul.

"I feed Claude sausages and cauliflower,"
said Maude. "And he loves to sip buttermilk
with a straw."

"What a strange diet for a tiger,"
thought Paul.

"Now it's time for your lunch, Paul,"
said Maude. "Here is a plate of dinosaur
scales with salted walnut sauce."

"Mmmm! My favorite!" squawked Paul.